LIFE WITH HARRY

Written by
Steffi Gardner

ISBN 978-1-914485-04-6

First Published November 2021

Designed, Printed & Published by Design Marque

Printed in Great Britain by www.designmarque.co.uk

LIFE WITH HARRY

Steffi Gardner

Foreword

I was delighted to learn that there is now a further instalment in the story of Harry's life (continuing on from "For Love of Harry").

This new book serves to show just what a slow and "up and down" process adoption and rehabilitation of a dog can be. In Harry's case, he is incredibly fortunate to have found a human who is knowledgeable, intuitive and determined to support him all the way. She is also willing and able to seek professional help alongside all of this where necessary.

I'd love anyone thinking of adopting a dog to read both these books to gain an insight to the support their new dog might need. Of course, many dogs move from home to home very smoothly, however those with a poor start in life like dear Harry often really, really struggle as you will read.

Hopefully with recent changes to legislation, puppy farms will be driven out of action and good breeders, who invest in their puppies' early experiences will be supported. Sadly, it is more likely that the only thing that will really achieve this is for people seeking a puppy to be educated about the damage done to puppies bred in puppy farms. It breaks my heart to see puppies being handed in to struggling rescues because their well-meaning people cannot cope with their additional needs.

Perhaps Harry's role in life is to educate people and make a true change for the better . . .

Morag Sutherland at Gelert Behaviour Training

Foreword

We have personally known the author, through our shared love of dogs.

My mum met her initially years ago at Langford Veterinary University, Bristol. They were both on the same course. In the breaks they got talking, and that's how the friendship began.

We all became friends and are still in close contact. Mum and I have extensive knowledge of dogs gained over many years as did my grandfather. Shared concerns about our dogs and others have forged close links over the years and continue to do so. Irrespective of whether our own dogs are concerned the author's knowledge and experience of alternative therapies has also been a welcome addition to our own knowledge. We have pooled our experiences and shared many a laugh and a joke over what initially some dog owners might regard as slightly way out thoughts. By this we mean the use of aromatics etc for animals.

When we heard Steffi was writing her first book about an ex puppy farm dog which she had adopted and called Harry we were delighted. She rang my mum on the day she decided to adopt him saying that mum must think she was mad. Mum disagreed. After all a dog in need. FOR LOVE OF HARRY was published in August 2020. We love it. It tells of Harry's struggles to adapt to a new life after six plus years on a puppy farm. Her second book LIFE WITH HARRY is due out later this year. We wouldn't be at all surprised to learn that a third is waiting in the wings!

Maureen and Marina Foley

Foreword

When we think about rescue dogs, we visualise an unwanted pet, stray or possibly abused in some way. But what many of us do not visualise is a rescue that has suffered more trauma, despair and isolation you could ever imagine.

'For the love of Harry' took you on a journey through the eyes of Harry a puppy farm survivor. How a frightened, nervous, untrusting rescue began to believe their was love and kindness in the world. Slowly but surely Harry started to come out of his shell with the very calm steady love that was given.

'Life with Harry', is a continuation of the journey with both Harry and his human family showing how in time patience and kindness will prevail.

This book shows how rewarding it can be when you adopt a rescue dog not always an easy task. It can sometimes take a long time for them to adjust, but when you see them running happily with joy on their faces that is reward enough.

Jan Houselander-Young

CHAPTERS

CHAPTER ONE

For Love of Harry was published in August 2020 and quite a lot has happened since I adopted him in 2019 including Covid with its restrictions.

Harry's progress has and at times continues to be slow, yet I have caught the glimmer of the odd breakthrough or two. How? Well, in Harry's case, the fact that he has looked as if he were processing things. At times like this he had, to my mind, the look of an old man, thinking about the past, bringing memories, both good and bad to the forefront of his mind as he looks again with fresh eyes on past events. Of course, with Harry, as with most ex-puppy farm dogs, we have no idea what is going on in their minds, so we can only surmise.

One of the curious things with Harry, and at first, I thought it was my imagination, is that when my friend from France telephones and she and I natter, he comes and listens. It is almost as if he understands French. Yes, probably ridiculous but there is something that attracts his attention! In October 2019, when I had him, the rescue only provided me with brief information about him. His chip was inserted in the UK, but a friend did wonder whether he had perhaps been bought by a foreign couple. Intriguing.

At the beginning of this year, January 2021, both Harry and I experienced a traumatic incident. It left both of us shocked and extremely upset. It was the totally unexpected death of my wonderful Golden Retriever, Tally. I was in the kitchen with her, and not away, which was a blessing. One minute she was standing by the door, the next she had collapsed. I stared stupidly at her lying on the floor, as I couldn't believe what was happening. Tally has been such an important part of both my life and Harry's, so I think it is only fitting that I pay tribute to her now.

Tally Guardian Angel
And Golden Girl

Tally unexpectedly left this earth at 8.30 am on Wednesday 27 January 2021. Thank God I was at home, up early, and with a little help from our neighbour Jeroen we were able to get her into the car. I raced to the vets but knew in my heart that any intervention would be too late. From the day I had her when she was four years old, this Golden Girl, a pale cream Retriever, there hadn't been one day that hasn't been filled with love and joy.

There is so much to remember about her from at times her obstinacy to her laughing face and eyes when she wanted a cuddle or came running back up the beach with a ball in her mouth. She adored sniffing and leaving her mark and though reluctant at times to go for a long walk that reluctance would change in an instant when we headed to the beach. She adored the water and would lie down in the sea no matter what time of year.

There's a small stream in the village that runs down the beach into the sea. One of my enduring memories is this. If she was too warm, she would trot up the beach, proudly carrying her ball, find a spot in the mix of sand and water she liked and lie down. She would then rise dripping, almost like Venus rising from the waves. However, unlike the goddess, Tally would need a shower when we got back home to get rid of the sand. Quite a task yet lovingly done.

She was a firm favourite at the groomers, yet as soon as she was home in the garden would roll in the grass often getting up with a stained face and head. There are no words to adequately describe Tally except to say that she exuded love from every pore. In October 2019 I adopted an extremely traumatised ex puppy farm dog from a rescue in Wales. A Miniature Schnauzer called Harry. He is probably five or six, maybe slightly older, and it is only thanks to Tally and her love that Harry is learning to love and to trust. She mothered him from the moment he was brought into the house, too terrified to move, letting him snuggle up to her, whether in her bed in the kitchen or in the lounge. She encouraged him to take his first tentative steps in the garden, then outside, and in every aspect of his life (read FOR LOVE OF HARRY) was his guardian angel.

Her sudden death this morning is inexplicable. She had just been fed and when I turned round, she was slumped on the floor, eyes glazed, front feet at an odd angle, breathing heavily. Her front legs were rigid. It has been suggested she may have been poisoned by something thrown over the garden wall. I pray it is not that as she would have been in agony. After the shock of her loss and thinking about the whole thing I am hoping to have either a post-mortem carried out or blood tests done. I am hoping I am wrong, and it was a massive, unexpected heart attack, but she was fitting when I arrived at the vets. If I am not wrong at least I can alert other dog owners to be more vigilant than ever. I was wrong!

We all know the feeling of devastation when our animals die. We know eventually it will happen. Harry knows she has gone. He has been looking for her. I have given him some Rescue Remedy to help his grief and bewilderment. He has tried to curl up to Crystal the spaniel, but she won't have any of it, so he now sits forlornly, looking for his buddy, his friend and to all intents and purposes his mum.

I'll carry the memory of Tally forever in my heart. My loving, joyful, exuberant golden girl, who gave so much and who was adored unconditionally. Run free!

CHAPTER TWO

Tally was the most remarkable dog I have ever come across. I miss her every single day but knowing she is over the rainbow bridge without pain, and I feel sure enjoying herself, helps to make the letting go easier.

I don't know how everyone thinks of their dogs that have passed over, but I feel if it is meant we do see them again when we too have passed. Enough of the maybes though, as this book concerns Harry and his life in the here and now.

He searched the house for her for a quite a while, looking puzzled, but I think Crystal the cocker spaniel made the loss less traumatic. Crystal has never been a dog that has wanted to interact with others. She has always had a "me, me, me"attitude, and been food possessive. That's another story. However, now at nearly twelve she has mellowed slightly though if she wants attention she just pushes herself in front of Harry! She is good at going out at night though and Harry normally follows her.

As I said earlier for a week following Tally's death I gave him Bach Rescue Remedy. How much that helped him I am not sure. There were no obvious outward signs. For instance he did not cry, but it was easy to see he was puzzled and down. I also offered him various oils and powders. I took the top off several, one at a time, but although he glanced at some, he did not appear to sniff any.   He did though re visit his old friend

Barley Grass. I put some in a saucer and he lapped the contents up, but after that when I put more down he ignored it.

How long it took him to adjust to Tally's loss I can't be sure. I mentioned in my previous book that he dislikes you looking at him so it was difficult to read from his body language, how he was holding himself, and what his body was telling me. He carried on eating, and drinking as normal, and was keen to go out on walks, so I went by that as a signal that he appeared to be coping. For several weeks I did not change the vet bed, thinking he might be getting some comfort from a familiar smell.

Sometimes I took him out on his own, at other times he and Crystal went out together. When on the beach he would run after a ball and always come back for his treats. Often over the fields off the lead he would run for a short distance then when I called him, ran back. At times I've been anxious and have wondered whether I was doing enough for him.

On reflection I think I am. I do sometimes forget, that unlike a young puppy with a 'clean sheet' Harry's baggage is unknown, ie he's had years of social deprivation. Therefore I must remember not to flood him with new ideas which he can't take in at once, and need to work at his own pace.

Through a friend I found about an holistic vet who is also a qualified homeopath. She practises in Carmarthenshire, not too far away, and her husband is also a vet, at another practice, where he works conventionally. I made an appointment and a copy of Harry's paperwork was sent over.

Of course Covid was about and travel somewhat restricted. However, due to the nature of the concern we were able to visit for a consultation. On the way there I stopped so Harry could do the necessary, and managed to find a supermarket where I could use the facilities and get a take-away drink. Harry with harness on lay on the back seat of the car and seemed oblivious to the ride, jumping down quite happily when we got to the nearest car park I could find.

As an aside, though you probably know, I read that we should really be lifting our dogs in and out of cars as it is not a good idea for them to junp down or in, as this puts strain on joints and ligaments, especially with larger dogs. As our dogs get older this can cause a variety of health issues.

I thought again of how I have stuck to an estate car for years, primarily because of the straight back, no lip to the boot, and the fact that it is relatively easy for me to bend down to lift up my dogs. Before Tally passed away I was on the point of buying a ramp which was solid enough to bear her weight happily and would hook on to the car. The things we dog owners need to consider when choosing a car!

Harry's consultation lasted two hours, though I had sent in a detailed sheet on him in advance. I was asked questions on the day too. Everything was gone through carefully, and Harry was allowed off the lead to explore the room. To our amazement he did nose around quite happily before coming back to sit at my side. A good point I gather. For quite some time the vet sat in her chair just glancing at Harry occasionally as she asked questions.

When the time came when she wanted to examine him she quietly and slowly got off her chair and sat on the floor. Nothing was rushed. Everything was calm and smooth. Harry had no objection to being touched which was great. Interestingly – he had some tiny black flecks on his coat. They looked like flea dirt but on closer inspection they weren't. What they were remains a mystery. He also had (and still does) a narrow strip of pale pinkish brown. This runs from the spine to the tail. I think I mentioned this in my previous book, so forgive me for repeating it. This strip appears to come and go.

It is faint and causes no problem. The vet couldn't say why it appears sometimes, then fades, at times to reappear. That's Harry!

The vet decided what to give Harry for starters. We both knew it could well take time for him to process things, and that another visit might be necessary. I was to keep a diary and e mail any changes over the next few months. Again, with homeopathy changes are made as the person or animal wishes, and what appears on the surface isn't always what is going on at a far deeper emotional level.

That's the same for us and from what I have read our thoughts, including the vibrations we send out often unknown to us, have a major effect on a dog's behaviour. If we are down hearted in any way our dogs will pick this up. Why? The simple fact, as I understand it, is that our body exudes certain chemicals and it is these changes in chemicals dogs respond to.

Sure you are all aware of this. If we are feeling fearful or anxious our dogs may well respond appropriately. I'll give you an instance. Harry is fine with people. However, recently he and I were out walking and someone came running towards us. This person, a male, was peculiarly dressed. I don't remember now what he was wearing but I do know I recoiled slightly. Harry lunged at him and of course I pulled him back. A few minutes later we met someone I know and I said 'Hello' and Harry walked on.

CHAPTER THREE

The time of Covid has brought many new things. On the down side the time frame of some of the events experienced by Harry may not be in precise date order.   For this I apologise

The more general reading about dogs I do, the more I begin to realise that although hard in the beginning thankfully most ex puppy farm dogs can and do settle into new homes, and that is wonderful. So much thanks has to be given to the marvellous foster families who initially look after these dogs at home, introducing them carefully to their own resident dogs and helping the newcomer get his or her first taste of normal family life. Amongst these are some people who are called 'failed fosterers!' They take in a rescue dog only to fall in love with it, and adopt it. Another happy ending.

Thanks though to the care and love of people who adopt rescue dogs the lives of these little souls are transformed completely. No longer abused but treasured and loved.   You only have to see the 'before'and 'after' photos posted by their new guardians to view these transformations.

Schnauzerfest is one of the rescues I support and I have 2022's calendar . The look of joy on the faces of the rescue dogs on this calendar is a delight. In some of the photos the dogs are racing about, having a great time. Others are happily resting.

When dogs are fostered if there is a resident happy relaxed dog chances are the newcomer will take its lead from this dog and find its safe place in the pecking order. There are other dogs some perhaps like Harry, where the trauma is so deep it will take a long time, occasionally years, before they can really settle. For most of us with a rescue dog the most important thing is that we have given a new life to an animal that has been so badly abused by people. These guardians have endless love and patience.

As every dog is an individual each will respond differently to different situations. I saw photos of a rescue bitch from Romania recently. Although she had been badly treated, unlike many, she was happily wagging her tail, which was wonderful to see. Many books on behaviour deal with nature v nurture. What is fascinating is that many breeding bitches will pass on to their offspring certain of their own characteristics.

Harry will be a mixture of his breeding and what he has learned/endured. There have been occasions when I was convinced his little brain isn't fully developped. Some things he appears to pick up quickly, whereas other relatively simple things he can't seem to process. But, does it really matter! I love him to bits and can't imagine life without him.

I was looking at photos I took of him back in 2019 when he was 'spaced out' and just standing by Tally, not daring to move. I look at him now lying in his bed in the lounge and although it was a massive blow for him when Tally died unexpectedly in January 2021 he is now settling, and actually seems to be gaining in confidence.

If I put on my socks and walking boots that is a signal to him that a walk is on the cards. He comes to sniff socks and boots, does a front body stretch, then back half stretch, sometimes with a yawn then follows me out to the kitchen. Yawns can indicate stress, but I am not seeing this. He knows walks mean titbits and sniffing and barks to go out of the door into the garden.

What is so wonderful to see is that if I have to go somewhere early and he knows his walk is not on the cards, there and then (you know that look) he comes into the room, sits down and you know the saying 'if looks could kill', well that is the look he gives me! Oh, I nearly forgot, a pugnacious look it is!

I've already (For Love of Harry) talked about the terror many of these ex puppy farm dogs have re doors and how doors are often used to trap them and worse. Harry still finds coming through doors difficult at times but we can live with that and gentle encouragement goes a long way. Even that seems to be improving slightly.

In her recent book 'Love is not Enough', Janetta Harvey talks about different ways of helping these ex puppy farm dogs.

Earlier I mentioned homeopathy, and how useful that can be. To help Harry even further I also consulted a suitably qualified behaviourist, an ex veterinary nurse, now a qualified dog behaviourist, and we had a two hour zoom session.

The questionnaire I was asked to complete and return beforehand, like the homeopathic vet's, was extensive. Apart from what you would expect, eg owner's knowledge of dogs, how long has the guardian/owner had dogs, breeds etc, whether previous dogs had received training, etc were questions about the dog's food.

The food we feed our dogs has a tremendous influence on their behaviour, as is how the food is absorbed by them, and what happens to the dog, both mentlly and physically (biome). The outcome of the consultation? I was pleased to find out I was doing so many of the things she recommended, including using techniques to help him feel at ease, to gain trust and to help with mental processing. Great news. At least I was getting something right!

For a while now I have been watching Raw Pet Medics on Facebook . I have found the programmes an eye opener. After listening to one programme on feeding for dogs I invested in a massive tome. The author Dr Conor Brady. The book Feeding Dogs - Dry or Raw? The science behind the debate. Probably not the stuff of bedtime reading if you want something to skip through.

It is interesting and thought provoking to see/hear what good quality food can achieve. I said previously I feed mostly raw food, with some fruit and vegetables, and a good probiotic, and I've always made bone broth for my dogs , from bones I get from the butcher. There are various recipes for making bone broth for dogs using uncooked bones, garlic, water and later herbs. It is cooked on low in a slow cooker for 24 hours and smells really good. The dogs love it.

For my dogs feeding this way works well, but others with perhaps an intolerance to certain foods, a different route might have to be followed. With this way of feeding and I can only speak for myself, my dogs' visits to the vets are rare. Yes there will always be times they need to go, but their vigour and quality of life to me is an indication of a good feeding regime.

Back to Harry. I have read several books written by people who have had rescue dogs, and some are far better than others, but I think that's the case in most disciplines. Personally, I still feel that helping Harry feel safe and trust in me is my number one priority no matter how long it takes. Having said that I need to address his reactive behaviour and disrupt this cycle. Part of this is changing my own view of what I expect. Rather like a self-fulfilling prophecy!

In the past on the beach, off the lead Harry has run part of the way towards off leash dogs, then turned back to me. I have always needed to be alert to call him back before he goes too far and perhaps out of his comfort zone. Having said that if they came to him off the lead even though they sniffed he has been fine with them and hasn't appeared worried.

CHAPTER FOUR

Young dogs are often exuberant and want to interact and often come dashing over. Had Harry been socialised as a puppy many of the behaviours he exhibits would have been dealt with at an early stage. Puppies with responsible guardians would have been off to training classes where their dogs would have learned socialisation with others and the first stage of training. Hopefully in a safe and positive environment. I did read somewhere that adult dogs can also benefit from training classes.

Unfortunately, Covid came along at a time when there were no training classes as such and I guess many of us muddled through.

Probably as an older dog, with maybe no training, changing patterns of established behaviours will always be far more difficult, and in some cases we have to accept that some behaviour/experiences are so ingrained it might only be possible to change them to some degree. You might think this is a defeatist attitude on my part. All I can say is that with Harry I am having to make considerable adjustments in my thinking and way of looking at things. One of which is positivity. Optimism not pessimism!

We are told taking our dog out every day is essential. However, advice seems to be changing and it is now thought some socialisation in the garden, with interaction and play time with the dog's guardian etc is equally important. Even sniffing to find dried food titbits is good. Harry loves this and as he sniffs more out on walks I have found this extends to his keeness to search for small treats in the garden. To see him engaging in this way makes me smile, especially when I look back to how 'switched off' he has been. Both he and Crystal know when titbits are being hidden and the eagerness with which they bound down the steps and run into the garden is evident. Food has always been one of Crystal's passions!

For Harry, the ringing of the doorbell was, until recently, a real issue. He would bark and it was a fear bark. Gradually the tone of his bark is changing and he is beginning to listen. Now when I ask him to go and lie down he often turns back from the door into the room. I think also that now he is more sure of himself and perhaps his role in the family, the vocalisation is him saying 'don't mess with me.' This is my place!

This might not seem like much, but believe you me for him it is quite a step. He is now far better at following and listening to hand and voice signals. Crystal the Cocker Spaniel at twelve is starting to wind down slightly and her barking at things in the home, often without cause, has increased. Added to this is the fact that she seems to be losing the ability to know when it is time for food in the afternoon. and will bark and bark until she is fed. Therefore, the fact that Harry is starting to listen and think for himself and not follow her lead is really positive.

I have a role to play here too in remembering not to raise my voice (I do sometimes forget of course). It has no effect on Crystal but Harry shrinks into himself. At times he has a questioning look in his eyes and I find myself watching his reactions and body language. Is he relaxed? Is he slightly tense wondering what is coming? Are his eyes and tail saying one thing but his body generally is saying something very different? I need to be aware of these things as I come to a closer understanding with him.

From time to time I fail, as tensions unknown to me come to the surface. Until recently if you looked at him he was not comfortable, and would turn his head away. As I'm writing this he has just raised his head from his bed to look at me. I wonder does he know I'm thinking of him? Has my body language altered? Possibly. He is breathing slowly and deeply and regularly, so he's obviously contented. Maybe I'm more relaxed too.

CHAPTER FIVE

We all know that smell plays an important part in a dog's life and cannot be under-estimated. Their lives are enriched by smells. I burned my hand slightly earlier this year and put on some lavender. I was not sitting near him but he could smell it and backed away to the far side of the room. As he relaxes in himself his smelling ability is becoming better.

Another small sign of trust beginning is the fact that when I dry him down after a bath or when he comes back from a walk wet, he now stands quite still and is relaxed, whether being dried in the bathroom or standing on the dog table. No more hunched body, eyes averted and stiffly held body.

A friend said recently that Harry is 'chubby' and wondered first of all was he being fed too much or was it something else. He still gobbles down his food but not as quickly and if he is starting to relax that will affect his digestive system. Certainly his rib cage has expanded and he has more strength in his limbs and moves better when he runs. I would say he is robust!

Something else I've noticed and I'm sure you will have too, is how we move and what this signals to our dogs. For instance how does Harry 'know' when I'm getting up to go to find his grooming box to look for a comb and edge away? There has to be something about my body language. Some sort of signal I give off? How does that differ from when I get up to go to the kitchen for a drink etc when he doesn't move a muscle?

A while ago I came across an interesting article in Science Direct. This talked about the association between behavioural problems in Brazilian dogs and the characteristics of both the dogs and their owners. It also mentioned the quality of owner-dog relationships. As an aside it is known that pheremones/ changes are detected by dogs. As our moods and thoughts change so do the pheremones we give out. That's just one scientific way to know that our dogs are able to smell changes in us.

I mentioned this before in FOR LOVE OF HARRY. With all those scent receptors it is no wonder they are ahead of the game. I need to return to the behaviourist I consulted as there was a great deal of information on her questionnaire I needed to process. All of this was ongoing and I thought we had cracked the problem when suddenly in Spring disaster struck.

CHAPTER SIX

It was on a Monday. Monday 31st May this year. My husband had taken the dogs for a walk . We walk up a long lane, turn left at the foottpath sign, and if the fields are empty let the dogs off the lead. It's a route we've all walked umpteen times before. They are able to run about freely and then are called back to have leads clipped back on before we get to the road. On this particular day Crystal came back but Harry wouldn't.

I had gone to the shops but knew as soon as I got back something was wrong. My husband and a neighbour were standing outside the house. John had a look of panic on his face; our neighbour's was full of concern. As I walked towards them John said that Harry had run away. He had run after him calling his name but Harry had fled. He had been seen crossing the main road and had run to the house but I wasn't there. He had then followed the walks we normally do and then disappeared. To say I was frantic is putting it mildly. Friends scoured the village, a neighbour first on his bike then by car, and others walked the route Harry might have taken, including the beach but he was nowhere to be seen. Much later when he was safely back at home someone said she had seen him on his own running away but had never thought to tell me. This person had been a dog owner! I couldn't believe it.

MISSING

HARRY

Male Schnauzer: Standard White (Age: Adult)

Missing from Broad Haven, Pembrokeshire, ran off when owner tried to put the lead back on , SA62 area, Wales on Monday, 31st May 2021

Harry is an ex puppy farm dog, wearing a collar with ID tag and Microchipped and Castrated. Can be scared of people but good with dogs off lead, not good with dogs on lead - DO NOT CHASE

CONTACT:

Help us find HARRY - print this poster from
https://www.doglost.co.uk/poster.php?dogId=167109

0844 800 3220

Doglost is a **FREE SERVICE** run by volunteers
www.doglost.co.uk
Reuniting Dogs with their Owners

Friends were marvellous, but nothing. John said that he didn't think Harry would have been taken as he wouldn't have let anyone near him. I must admit it was scant consolation. My mind seemed to be on auto pilot.

Sure you can imagine the thoughts coursing through my mind. Try as he might John couldn't think of any reason why Harry would have taken off as he did. We've been over and over that day and still have no idea why he ran away.

CHAPTER SEVEN

I made up posters and they were put up locally and on Facebook. Out and about I talked to as many people as possible showing them his picture and telling them that he was a rescue dog. I explained that he would be terrified, and asked if they did see him would they mention it in the local shops.

A dog rescue rang (DOGLOST). They are a free service run by volunteers; their aim is to reunite dogs with their owners. They asked for a photo so they could post his details online. Guess what, they knew of someone with a drone which might be useful.

Unfortunately, the wind was too high for the drone to be flown safely but the fact that there were people out there looking for him was a real help, though I couldn't rest. The rescue I had him from rang. They had heard what had happened.

I had to go through the story and was given some advice including to go out at dawn and dusk to the area where he had run away. I was to sit quietly and he might return. He wouldn't have gone far. He had in fact covered over 4 miles. The times given were the best as Harry would probably be hiding somewhere close by during the day, but would venture out when it was quiet. The rescue said to get in touch with them day or night if I needed to and update them, which I did.

So at dawn with Crystal in tow I retraced Harry's route and sat quietly in the field hoping! Someone from an independent rescue society suggested I use an old pair of tights and put spiced meatballs in them and trail that over the ground and down the lane. Sometimes dogs would follow the scent of food. I did that thinking it was just as well I lived in a rural area as anyone in a built up area seeing a woman out at dawn trailing a pair of tights behind her would have had serious misgivings about that person's sanity!

Crystal was quiet and lagged behind, not like her. You have probably guessed what was happening. I turned back to see where she was to find she had made a hole in the tights and was eating the meatballs!

Walking down the lane in the early morning I could hear Harry somewhere in the distance crying. I was at really low ebb then. He was obviously in distress and I remember calling his name, in the vain hope he could hear me. I had to do something and as I couldn't locate the sound except that it seemed to be somewhere away to my left I wanted him to be aware of the fact I was searching for him.

It probably did no good whatsoever for him, but it helped me a lot. I kept thinking of how terrified he must be and other things too! Where was he? The only positive thing was that the weather during those few days was dry so wherever he was hiding he wouldn't be wet and cold. I had to keep these thoughts in my mind.

I drove to various farms and houses, leaving posters. At one place a local fisherman had seen a small white dog but it had dashed past him and he had been unable to catch it. I remember thinking why oh why had he not done anything about it as he must have realised the dog was on his own and terrified. I thought later that thought was unfair because who would he have contacted. It's not a matter that concerns the police.

On the Wednesday morning I had a call from a local farmer's wife. She had heard about Harry and was concerned. In the past she had lost two of her dogs. I gather they had been shot by a farmer as they were in with his sheep. A farmer of course has every right to shoot stray dogs to protect his livestock. She didn't want the same thing to happen to us.

She gave me the telephone number of someone nearby, a local farmer who had sheep. I rang and explained the position. ie Harry was an ex puppy farm rescue dog who for some reason had run away from my husband during a walk. I explained that Harry was small and white, would have no idea where he was and I was concerned that he might be in with his sheep. The farmer went to look and rang back to say that his sheep were fine and there was no sign of Harry.

The lady concerned had also asked me if I had taken a poster of Harry to a camp site on a nearby farm. I hadn't so off John and I went and left a poster. Later we had a call saying a small dog had been seen once and had been crying for two nights, much to the annoyance of many of the campers. We drove over there and I explained the situation. The camp site owner's attitude completely changed as he could see what distress we were in.

As we stood talking we saw a man nearby filling a large container with water. He came across and said that he and his son in law had heard a dog barking and it sounded distressed. They had decided that if he was still barking that night they would go out when it was dark with head torches on, and search until they found him.

At that moment a call came in on the farmer's mobile to say a small white dog had been seen in a nearby field. The lady calling was going towards him with her own dog, in the hope the other would come towards them. Of course he was so terrified he just ran away. In the distance I could see a shape, a white shape running away. In vain I called his name, but the last view I had of him was him disappearing through a rickety gate which led into a deeply wooded valley, strewn with trees, and brambles etc.

CHAPTER EIGHT

By now I was desperate. So near yet so far away. I was shaking. I was inconsolable. I just wanted him home. At least I knew Harry was ok and not hurt or trapped anywhere. Maybe if I camped out overnight near where I had seen him disappear he would come back. John went home to find a tent etc and as he went I saw coming towards me two men, one of whom I had met earlier, with a lady and two children.

We all stood talking then to my amazement both men went in through the broken gate and down into the densely wooded valley below. One went right, the other left. I could hear rotten branches cracking and was concerned the men might fall and be hurt. However, Phil said that her husband and her father revelled in this type of 'boys own' work and would probably enjoy the search.

The whole family were so kind. It was unbelievable. The children lifted my spirits up as they asked about Harry and I explained about his distressing past. Phil explained that as a family they had taken in various rescue animals at different times, so I felt we had a bond between us.

I had a feeling though that the men would return empty handed. They did. When they reappeared they said that they had seen him but he had run away. However, they had found where he had been sleeping as he had circled and made a small bed in the grass.

Again I was so thankful there had been no rain for several days. Thanks to the maps on their I phones they had a good idea where he was heading. They had seen him climb a steep bank in the woods and reckoned he would come out at the bottom of a garden on a neighbouring farm. We walked back through a field to the camp site and Phil offered to make some tea and brought a camping chair for me to sit on. I decided to wait for John, but it was their unbelievable kindness that almost had me in tears.

John returned. We had a cup of tea and after thanking everyone I drove off heading in what I hoped was the right direction. I explained to the farm owner we knew about Harry and asked if we could cross his garden and go into the woods. He didn't seem that happy when I mentioned I would perhaps camp out that night; but who can blame him!

We squeezed through the partially open gate and waited. I could hear Harry crying. *I s*ay cry but it sounded like a sob and it would have been had it come from a person. It was the sound made by someone who feels abandoned and alone. Someone who had given up all hope of being rescued. It was pitiful to hear. In fact heart breaking. The sound though was much nearer.

There was nothing I could do but pray. I couldn't face the consequences of not finding him. All I could think of was him and what he had gone through. The rescue had said not to call him by name, nor chase him as he would be so disorientated he would just run. I waited praying he would come to me; would recognise me. The bushes nearby rustled and a cry came again. Then silence.

'Look what I've got – sweeties' I called in as calm and positive a tone of voice as I could, though my hands holding the bag of liver treats was shaking. We saw and heard bushes move again, nearer this time , coupled with another cry. I called the same words once more shaking the bag. Neither John nor I dared move.

It was John who spotted the little white head first as he whispered to me 'look he's there. Can you see him?' I looked at where he was pointing as slowly, so slowly, a little head emerged. Harry stared at me, his eyes unfocused. So I repeated the words again 'Look what I've got, holding out a treat on the palm of my hand. He hesitated, unsure, then took a slow tentative step forward. I can't describe my thoughts. A miracle was happening before my eyes. Sure anyone who has lost a dog only to be reunied with it will know exactly what I mean. I took out another treat and this time he edged slightly nearer. I extended my hand slowly and managed to grasp his collar and immediately clipped on his lead. He then had another treat before I turned away with him following. I couldn't believe it. Relieved. To say I was relieved was an under-statement. 'He's safe, he's safe, he's safe' I kept saying to myself. The nightmare had ended.

Harry chuntered all the way back to the car. It was like music to my ears. He seemed to be telling me off that I had lost him. Where had I been? I couldn't stop smiling to myself and could hardly believe I had him safe and sound. 'The farmer was incredulous too! I had lifted Harry into the car intending to put him on the back seat. But he beat me to it. He clambered up onto the seat, did a few little turns then lay down on the vet bed. Exhausted. The sight of his little legs as he'd scrambled up was indescribable. I gazed at him, joy filling my heart. I drove back to the camp site, found Phil and family and gave them the good news. Their faces lit up. The following day I returned with something as a thank you. Something for the whole family to enjoy! I can never repay them for their kindness. Truly they were incredible as were friends and neighbours. Back at home Crystal merely sniffed him before wandering away in search of food.

So Harry, where do we go from here? In many ways he has lost a lot of ground. I had been able to let him off the lead before on both the beach and the boardwalk sure he would come back when I called him. Now he is on a longline, but at least he won't run off. Sometimes if the beach is empty I will let him off for a few minutes and occasionally he will run after a ball. However, he will suddenly stop and look around in panic. There is an unfocussed look in his eyes. I can see it coming and quickly pick up the longline. I don't know what it is that scares him but scared he is as his tail goes down and he can't wait to leave the beach. Now I need to be the strong one, strong and positive for him, take over the role Tally played.

We bought Harry a tracker, just in case, but if it is switched on (just to test it) he hates the sound. He is apprehensive and his tail goes down. On walks he is happy to sniff, and in the garden as I said I hide small treats and he and Crystal can hardly wait to dash down the steps searching for these.

Something really positive that has happened over the last six weeks or so is that sometimes he will come to the settee and put his front legs up. I do some TTouch work with him leaving him free to decide when he has had enough. He has started to do this with John too, though I'm not sure whether it is for a small piece of banana or not. Still what does it matter!

He goes to puppy day care from time to time, with the lady who home boards him and Crystal if we are away. Apparently he enjoys himself. If the two are there Crystal just goes somewhere she can relax and snooze. On Sunday 26 September, there were national Schnauzerfest walks. We went to our local one, Harry and I. Although the forecast showed fine weather it drizzled part way through. We did an early walk with another lady with her rescue Mini Schnauzer Bonnie and when we got back to the car park others had arived with dogs in tow. Not all Mini Schnazers but all in support of Schnauzerfest.   In the end I didn't take him on the full walk but it was good he had done a meet and greet with some. His legs were trembling slightly but he did settle down and safely back in the car he went to sleep.

CHAPTER NINE

It does seem he is coming out of his shell a little more. John and I had a few days holiday and when I rang to check how the dogs were doing was told Harry was slightly more vocal. Was it time for another layer of the onion to be peeled off?

He does appear to be a little more confident in himself, though if I am out of the room for too long he comes to check where I am. He is still reactive at times to other dogs but can usually be distracted.

I look at him from time to time as he lies in his bed apparently asleep. I know I was so lucky to find him, and he and I are forging a bond of trust. We are moving forward albeit slowly, but as I've said before time really doesn't matter.

What is important is that good memories are beginning to replace bad. I would love to find him a companion, a playmate with whom he can form a doggy bond. I have looked but so far although I thought I had found the ideal companion for different reasons it hasn't happened.

Maybe I have to wait and trust that when the time is right, just as I was led to find him back in October 2019 I will be guided to the right one for him.

© Stefanja (Steffi) Gardner November 2021.

Printed in Great Britain
by Amazon